Foreward

We are born with our eyes and our hearts wide open. Innocence and youth make it so easy to believe...so easy to fall asleep in someone's arms, to trust in smiles, to see animals float across the sky...to believe your summer will never end.

This gift that we're given - to not just hope - but truly believe in people and feelings and all these things under the sun...this ability to act like it all matters...where does that gift go? Why does time and experience have to wear it away, instead of building on it? At what point do we lose the courage to believe and then just start hoping? And why do some give up completely?

Now, I am not the most courageous of sorts...but I'm not willing to give up this most precious gift, for me or for you. I know it won't be easy, and I know it shouldn't be. And I'm going to fight for it, everyday. Because inside this beautiful struggle to believe, we are given the power to comfort, to heal, to inspire and to love.

As I get older, I know my summers may not last forever, but I'm not going to stop believing in the chances that rise with each morning sun. And I know it matters...it always does...the things we do, the things we say, the lives we lead, and the hearts we touch.

I want to see giraffes float by, instead of gray clouds, I want to feel the sun, deep inside of me, even when it isn't shining...I have to believe in myself enough to have the courage to say "I love you," and mean it...and have the strength to hear "I love you" and really feel it.

I believe all this can happen for me, and I believe it can happen for you.

To Ned, Brett, David and always, Mom -
the voices that whisper in my ear and tell me, not only what is,
but what can be, and I believe them.

Waldman House Press is an imprint of TRISTAN Publishing, Inc.

Waldman House Press
2300 Louisiana Avenue North, Suite B
Golden Valley, MN 55427

Copyright © 2003, Jodi Hills
ISBN 0-931674-52-2
Printed in China
First printing

Library of Congress Cataloging-in-Publication Data

Hills, Jodi, 1968-
Believe / written & illustrated by Jodi Hills.
p. cm.
ISBN 0-931674-52-2 (alk. paper)
1. Conduct of life. I. Title.

BJ1581.2.H546 2003
170'.44--dc21   2003054350

To Mary –
I believe in you!

Believe

jodi hills

Waldman House Press
Minneapolis, MN

It isn't that something comes along and gives
you a reason to get out
of bed...

I believe you have to get out of bed and
go find
that
reason - *everyday.*

I believe that some days the sun lights my path
a little brighter than others,
but it always gives me a *chance.*

And in that chance,
I have to believe
my feet will take me where I need to go.

I believe, along the way,
there are some people that you have to let in,
and there are some you have to let go...

and believe me,
one is not necessarily easier than the other.

I believe we don't always
get what we ask for,

and so often we're *lucky* we don't.

I believe that everything happens for a reason,

but I rarely have the *patience*
to wait
for the
understanding...

even though I believe patience is a virtue,
I fear it isn't one of mine.

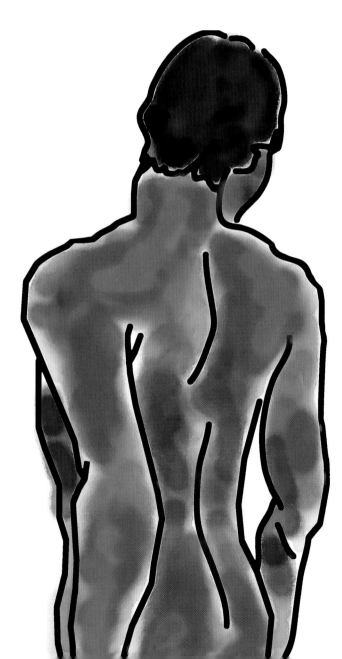

I believe there is no bravery
without being afraid.

Yet I'm afraid
that I'm not always brave
enough to let others know how I feel.

I believe that I'm not an easy person to *love*,

but believe me,
I'd love
you to try.

I believe in the pure
randomness of it all.
I believe that no one escapes.
And I take comfort in the fact
that it could happen to anyone
at any time...
pain,
confusion,
happiness,

even love.

I believe there is no greater wealth than *happiness.*

And I believe that the wealth must be *shared.*

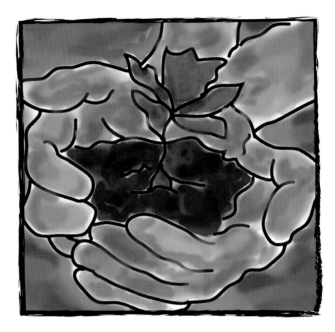

I believe that tears and laughter can both be *healthy.*

I believe in the power of attitude over illness.

I believe a

smile

can heal,

and one should be given to every face,
and every mirror.

And I believe your face
should always show what's in your heart.

I believe that

"please"

and

"thank you"

are still the
"magic words."

But I think the words,

"I believe in you"

may be
the most magical
of all.

I believe in myself,
only because you believed in me first,
and because of that,
I may not always be

safe,

but I will be

saved.

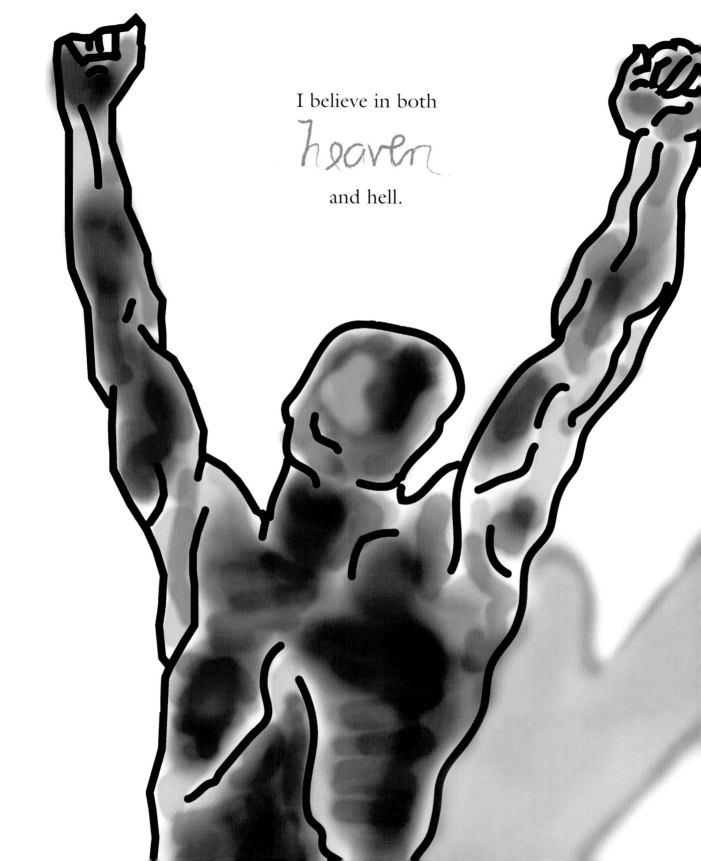

I believe in both

heaven

and hell.

I seem to travel
through both
on nearly a daily
basis.

And I believe
I could not
know one
without the
other.

I believe that I could

win or lose,

that I could fall, or rise,
at any given moment.

I believe the only way I fail, is if I don't try.

I believe there's so much more than just
"good enough." And I believe that perfection
knows no time constraints.   For whatever
time I've been given with you, has been a

perfect gift.

I believe
you have to
prepare yourself for the *best.*

You have to believe
it's ok to hope for it,
work for it
and embrace it when it comes.

And I believe you need
to help others do the same.

I believe that without knowledge or permission,
our lives become entangled,
and not always for the easier, but so often,

for the better.

I believe that we're all just looking
for those reasons to get out of bed,
to find a well lit path, to be happy,

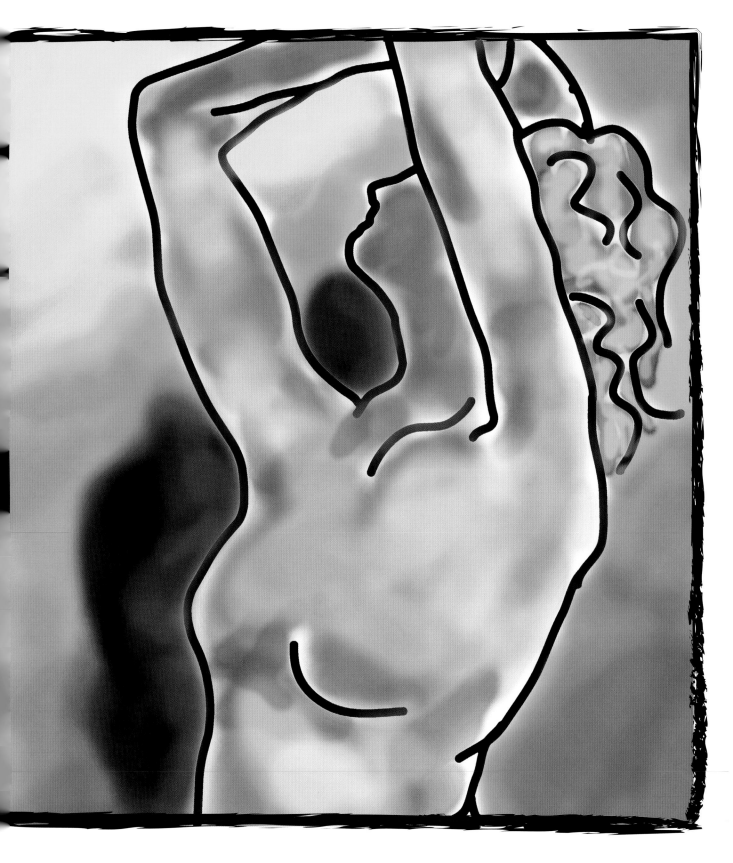

You are not my sole reason...
I don't believe anyone can be,
or should be asked to be...
but you're
a good reason...

a good reason

to believe
in something, and in someone.

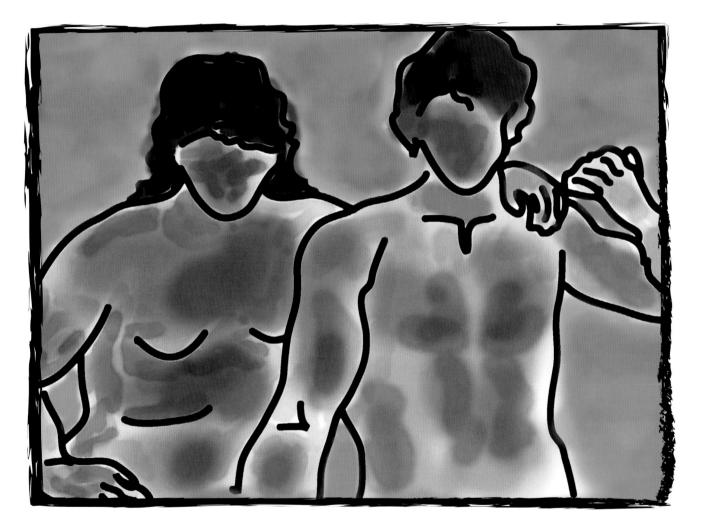

And just so you know
that some

magic

is still real...

"thank you" for believing in me..

and "please" believe me
when I tell you, that

"I believe in you."

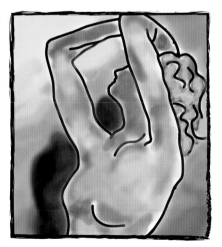

"I believe in you" "I believe in
you" "I believe in
believe in you" "I believe
"I believe in you"
"I believe in you" "I believe in you
you" "I believe in you"
"I believe in you"
"I believe in you" "I believe

"I believe in you" "I believe in you" "I believe in you" "I believe in you" "I believe in you" "I believe in you" "I believe in you" "I believe in you" "I believe in you" "I believe in you" "I believe